# TERRIFIC TRAINS

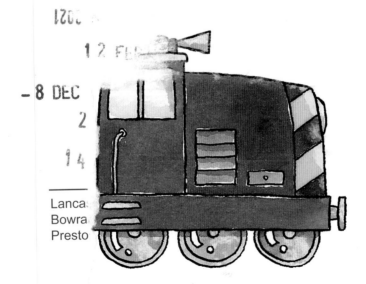

*For Mandy, John, Chloe and Charlie – T.M.*
*For Gorran – A.P.*

First published 1998 by Kingfisher
This edition published 2014 by Macmillan Children's Books
a division of Macmillan Publishers Limited
20 New Wharf Road, London N1 9RR
Basingstoke and Oxford
Associated companies throughout the world
www.panmacmillan.com

ISBN: 978-1-4472-5075-3

1 3 5 7 9 8 6 4 2

A CIP catalogue record for this book
is available from the British Library.

Printed in China

# TERRIFIC TRAINS

Tony Mitton
and
Ant Parker

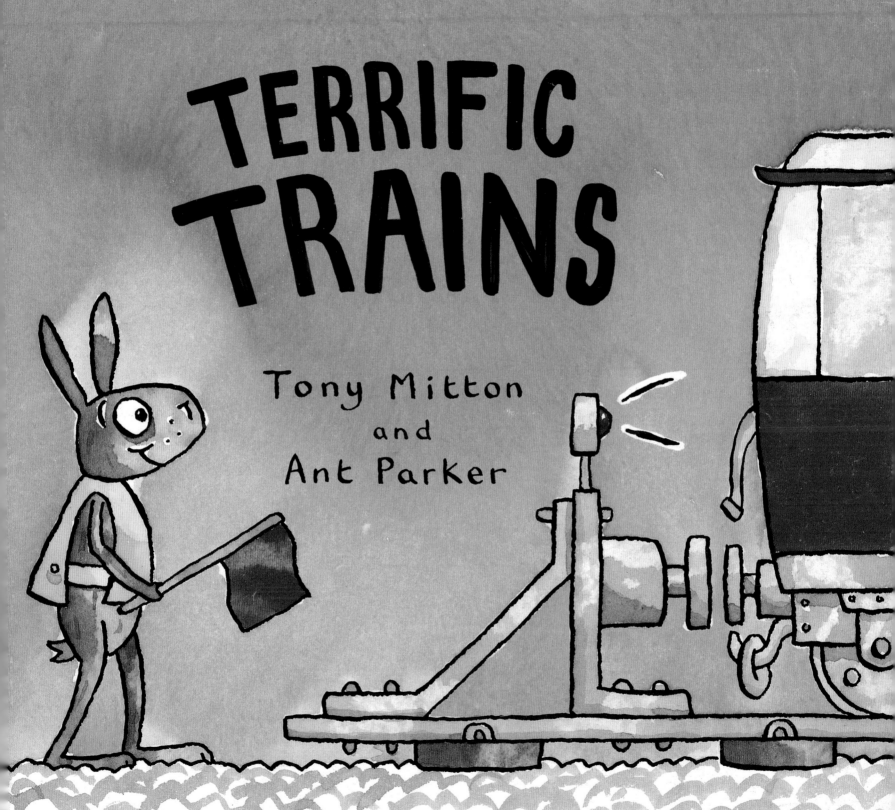

MACMILLAN CHILDREN'S BOOKS

Big trains, small trains, old trains and new,

rattling and whistling – choo, choo, choo!

Starting from the station with a whistle and a hiss,

steam trains puffing and chuffing like this.

Diesel trains rushing as they rattle down the line,

warning us they're coming with a long, low whine.

Metal wheels whirl as they whizz along the track.
They shimmer and they swish
with a slick click-clack.

Carriages are coupled in a neat, long chain.
An engine pulls the carriages,
and that makes a train.

If a train meets a river or a valley or a ridge,

the train goes over on a big, strong bridge.

If a train meets a mountain it doesn't have to stop.

It travels through a tunnel and your ears go pop!

When too many trains try to share the same track,

the signals and the points have to hold some back.

When the rail meets a road,
there's a crossing with a gate.

The train rushes through
while the traffic has to wait.

Trains travel anytime, even very late.

This train's delivering a big load of freight.

This train's for passengers.
We'll soon be on our way.

All aboard and wave goodbye –
we're off on holiday!

# Train bits

## rails

electric rail

these are metal strips that form a pathway called a **track** or **railway line** – some trains get their power from an electric rail

## whistle

this makes a noise to warn everyone that the train is coming

## signal

this tells train drivers when to stop and go

## wagon

this is for carrying goods, called **freight**

## carriage

this is for carrying people, called **passengers**

## points

these are rails that move to let the railway line divide so the train changes direction